A Picture Book of

CATS

Written by Joanne Mattern
Illustrated by Roseanna Pistolesi

Troll Associates

WHITE PERSIAN

This beautiful, long-haired cat is one of the most popular *breeds*, or types. Its thick fur and stocky body give this cat an impressive appearance.

Some Persian cats have orange or copper eyes. Others have blue eyes. And some have one eye of each color!

Owning a Persian can be a lot of work. Their long fur must be brushed every day to keep it looking nice. And because they have such squashed-in faces, these cats sometimes have trouble breathing. But they make beautiful and loving pets, and many people enjoy their company.

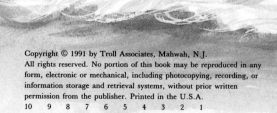

Library of Congress Cataloging-in-Publication Data

Mattern, Joanne, (date)
    A picture book of cats / written by Joanne Mattern; illustrated by Roseanna Pistolesi.
        p.   cm.
    Summary: Describes several types of cats, including the Persian, Tabby, and Sphynx.
    ISBN 0-8167-2146-7 (lib. bdg.)   ISBN 0-8167-2147-5 (pbk.)
    1. Cat breeds—Juvenile literature.   2. Cats—Pictorial works—Juvenile literature.   [1. Cats.   2. Cat breeds.]   I. Pistolesi, Roseanna, ill.   II. Title.
SF445.7.M27   1991
636.8—dc20   90-42548

CORNISH REX

The Cornish Rex's curly coat makes it look different from other cats. Most cats have two types of fur. The outer coat is made of stiff *guard* hairs. These protect the cat. The inner coat, or *undercoat,* is made of *down* hairs. These keep the cat warm. But the Cornish Rex has no visible guard hairs. This makes its fur soft and wavy. Its whiskers are curly, too!

This breed has only been around since about 1950. They make very loving and friendly pets.

SCOTTISH FOLD

In 1961, a cat was found in Scotland whose ears folded forward and down. Soon, more of these cats were born, and the Scottish Fold became a new breed of cat. It is one of the newest breeds.

When a Scottish Fold is born, its ears look just like any other cat's. But when it is about a month old, the kitten's ears begin to fold forward. They stay this way for the rest of the cat's life.

DOMESTIC SHORTHAIRS

These cats have something in common with many people in the United States. Their ancestors came to this country as immigrants. In fact, this is the oldest *domesticated*, or pet, cat in America. Some people think these cats even traveled on the *Mayflower!*

Domestic Shorthairs can be any color. Some have tabby markings or are a mixture of several colors. They are usually strong, smart, and loving cats. People once depended on these cats to catch mice and rats. Now they are favorite family pets and companions.

BRITISH BLUE

Pet this lovely cat and you may think you are touching a stuffed toy. The British Blue's fur is short and plush. It feels very soft and thick.

The British Blue is much admired in England, and though they are not very common, you will often see them in cat shows there. They are very intelligent, quiet animals, and make very good pets.

SILVER TABBY

A *Tabby* is a cat whose fur is marked with dark stripes or blotches on a light background. Many cats have these kinds of markings. Tabbies can be brown, red, blue, cream, or silver. A silver is the least common type of Tabby.

The word "tabby" comes from the city of Attabiya in the Middle East. Long ago, people in that city made silk cloth with a pattern that looked like the Tabby's coat.

SIAMESE

If you have a Siamese cat for a pet, you may feel it owns *you!* This cat is very smart and likes people to pay attention to it. Siamese cats often ''talk'' in loud yowls.

Siamese always have blue eyes. The kittens are all white when they are born. The dark markings on their face, legs, and tail don't show up until they are older.

These cats originally came from a country called Siam. (Today this country is known as Thailand.) They were pets of the royal family. In 1884, two cats named Pho and Mia were brought to England. Today the Siamese is one of the most popular cats.

MANX

This cat is missing something—its tail! There is just a small hollow where the tail should be. It is the only cat that has no tail. The Manx also has hind legs which are longer than its front legs. This makes the cat run with a quick, bouncy step, almost like a rabbit's hop.

Manx cats are very smart. They like to play, and make very good pets.

SPHYNX

This rare and unusual cat has hardly any hair. Only a little bit of short, thin fur covers parts of its body. Even its whiskers aren't as long as other cats' are. A hairless kitten that was born in Canada in 1966 was the start of this new breed. Because of that, this breed is sometimes called the Canadian Hairless.

The Sphynx has so little fur that it is hard for it to keep warm. It loves to lie in the sun or in front of a radiator, soaking up the heat.

CALICO

The black, brown, and orange patches of fur on a white background that make this cat so interesting to look at also gave the Calico its name. "Calico" is a kind of cloth that is often spotted with many bright colors—just as this cat is.

Calicos are usually very good mothers. They enjoy playing with and caring for their very colorful kittens, and like to keep the kittens with them until they are quite big.

SPOTTED CAT

Several wildcats are spotted, including the cheetah and the jaguar. But only one kind of domesticated cat is. The Spotted Cat is thought to be one of the oldest breeds of cat. People have found drawings of it that are several thousand years old.

The spots on this cat can be many different shapes, from round to star-shaped. Sometimes one cat will have several different kinds of spots. Most Spotted Cats are brown or silver, but they can also be red, cream, or even blue.

KITTENS

No matter what breed a cat is, it started out as a kitten. About 3-5 kittens are born in each *litter*, or group of young. They are blind and deaf until they are about 2 weeks old. Their mother cares for them until they are about 2 months old.

Kittens are lots of fun to play with. It is interesting to watch them grow up and turn into—cats!